Super Simple
Move & Shake

Healthy & Fun Activities to Move Your Body

Nancy Tuminelly

Contributing Physical Education Consultant, Linn Ahrendt, Power Play Education, Inc.
Consulting Editor, Diane Craig, M.A./Reading Specialist

A Division of ABDO

ABDO
Publishing Company

visit us at www.abdopublishing.com

Published by ABDO Publishing Company, a division of the ABDO Group, P.O. Box 398166, Minneapolis, Minnesota 55439. Copyright © 2012 by Abdo Consulting Group, Inc. International copyrights reserved in all countries. No part of this book may be reproduced in any form without written permission from the publisher. Super SandCastle™ is a trademark and logo of ABDO Publishing Company.

Printed in the United States of America, North Mankato, Minnesota
052011
092011

 PRINTED ON RECYCLED PAPER

Editor: Liz Salzmann
Content Development: Nancy Tuminelly, Linn Ahrendt
Cover and Interior Design and Production: Colleen Dolphin, Mighty Media, Inc.
Photo Credits: Colleen Dolphin, Shutterstock

The following manufacturers/names appearing in this book are trademarks:
Elmers® Glue-All™

Library of Congress Cataloging-in-Publication Data

Tuminelly, Nancy, 1952-
  Super simple move & shake : healthy & fun activities to move your body / Nancy Tuminelly.
    p. cm. -- (Super simple exercise)
  ISBN 978-1-61714-961-0
  1. Physical fitness for children--Juvenile literature. I. Title.
  GV443.T857 2012
  613.7'042--dc22
                                                              2011000978

Note to Adults

This book is all about encouraging children to be active and play! Avoid having children compete against each other. At this age, the idea is for them to have fun and learn basic skills. Some of the activities in the book require adult assistance and/or permission. Make sure children play in appropriate spaces free of objects that can cause accidents or injuries. Stay with children at the park, playground, or mall, or when going for a walk. Make sure children wear appropriate shoes and clothing for comfort and ease of movement.

Contents

Time to Move & Shake!

Being active is one part of being healthy. You should move your body for at least one hour every day! You don't have to do it all at one time. It all adds up.

Being active gives you **energy** and helps your body grow strong. There are super simple ways to move your body. Two of them are moving and shaking. This book has fun and easy activities to get you started. Try them or make up your own.

Do You Know?
Being Active Helps You

1 be more relaxed and less stressed

2 feel better about yourself and what you can do

3 be more ready to learn and do well in school

4 rest better and sleep well at night

5 build strong bones, **muscles**, and joints

So turn off the TV, computer, or phone. Get up and start moving and shaking!

Muscle Mania

You have **muscles** all over your body. You use them whenever you move any part of your body. The more you move your muscles, the stronger they get!

arm

neck

shoulder

stomach

chest

back

upper leg

lower leg

Healthy Eating

You need **energy** to move your body. Good food gives your body energy. Some good foods are fruits, vegetables, milk, lean meat, fish, and bread. Foods such as pizza, hamburgers, French fries, and candy are okay sometimes. But you shouldn't eat them all the time.

Remember!

- ☑ Eating right every day is as important as being active every day
- ☑ Eat three healthy meals every day
- ☑ Eat five **servings** of fruits and vegetables every day
- ☑ Eat healthy snacks
- ☑ Eat fewer fast foods
- ☑ Drink a lot of water
- ☑ Eat less sugar, salt, and fat

Move It Chart

Make a chart to record how much time you spend doing things. Put your chart where you will see it often. This will help you remember to fill it out every day. See if you move your body at least an hour each day.

Activity	Sunday	Monday	Tuesday	Wednesday	Thursday	Friday	Saturday
tennis	●		●	●	●		●
Freeze Frame		●				●	
pull weeds			●				

1. Put the title of your chart at the top of a piece of paper. Then put "Week of" and a line for the dates.

2. Make a chart with eight **columns**. Put "activity" at the top of the first column. Put the days of the week at the top of the other columns. Under "activity," list all of the things you do. Include sports, games, and **chores**. Don't forget the activities in this book! Put "total time" at the bottom. Make copies of the chart.

3. Start a new chart each week. Put the dates at the top.

4. Mark how much time you spend on each activity each day. Be creative! Use different colors, **symbols**, or clock faces. For example, a blue sticker could mean 15 minutes of movement. A purple sticker could mean 60 minutes of movement.

- ◗ = 10 minutes
- ● = 15 minutes
- ◯ = 30 minutes
- ⬤ = 60 minutes

5. Add up each day's activity. Did you move your body at least an hour every day?

Tools & Supplies

Here are some of the things you will need to get started.

music player

thick paper plates

plastic bowls

bucket

tape measure

scissors

clear tape

markers

empty shoebox

glue

construction paper

uncooked pasta

stapler

masking tape

ribbon

paper streamers

metal lid

music

toilet paper tubes

broom

sticks

paper towel tube

11

Copycat Charades

How does your favorite animal dance?

WHAT YOU NEED

paper

markers

music player

favorite music,
  jungle theme if possible

MUSCLES USED

leg

arm

shoulder

stomach

back

neck

TIME

10-15 minutes

1. Write a list of animals on a piece of paper.

2. Someone says the first animal on the list and starts the music. Everyone moves the way the animal moves. How does the animal move? Run? Jump? Move its head? Play? Try different moves for the animal.

3. Stop the music. Everyone stops moving.

4. Someone says the next animal on the list. Start the music. Move like that animal.

5. Keep going until you've done all of the animals on the list.

➡ Try having everyone dance like their favorite animal. Hold a copycat party where everyone moves like their animal for one song.

Freeze Frame

No two moves are ever the same!

WHAT YOU NEED

music player
different kinds of music

MUSCLES USED

leg
arm
shoulder
neck

TIME

10-15 minutes

1. Start the music. Everyone moves in a way that feels like the song.

2. Swing your arms. Twist your body. Bend your knees. Kick your legs. Make up funny big and small moves. Make faces with your mouth and eyes to match the music.

3. **Freeze** when the music stops. Do not move. Stay where you are. If your leg is in the air, keep it up. Anyone who moves is out of the game.

4. Start the music again. Play the music for different lengths of time. Keep going until only one person is left in the game.

5. It's fun to see how many different kinds of moves you can make. Try to use all parts of your body.

➡ This is a good activity to do before you have to sit for a long time.

Hokey Pokey

A favorite activity that everyone loves!

WHAT YOU NEED

....

open space with nothing
   in the way
music player
"Hokey Pokey" song
   or other lively music

MUSCLES USED

....

leg
arm

TIME

....

10-15 minutes

1. Stand in a circle facing each other.

2. Play the "Hokey Pokey" song and practice the moves. Each **verse** is about a different body part.

> *Put your right foot in.*
> *Put your right foot out.*
> *Put your right foot in and*
> *   you shake it all about.*
> *Do the hokey pokey and*
> *   you turn yourself around.*
> *That's what it's all about!*

3. Now do the same with your elbows!

4. Next try it with your knees!

5. Keep doing the same with as many parts as you can. Don't forget your hands, hips, shoulders, head, back, side, and whole self.

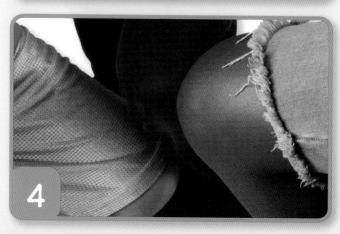

17

TV Busters!

A good way to get tired watching TV!

WHAT YOU NEED

paper
markers or crayons
empty shoe box
TV

MUSCLES USED

leg
arm
shoulder
stomach
back

TIME

1-5 minutes

1 Write different exercises on sheets of paper. Use the suggestions below or think of your own! Then fold each paper. Put them all in the box. These are the TV Busters.
- Jumping Jacks
- Run in place
- Hop on one foot
- Jump up and touch the floor
- Front kicks, side kicks, back kicks
- Knee bends
- Arm circles
- **Punch** the air with your fists
- Sit-ups

2 Watch TV. At each **commercial** break, pick a TV Buster from the box. Read it out loud.

3 Everyone jumps up and does the exercise until the show starts again.

19

Romp 'n' Stomp

Make instruments out of everyday objects!

WHAT YOU NEED

plastic bowls
buckets
metal lids
brooms
sticks

MUSCLES USED

leg
arm
shoulder

TIME

10-15 minutes

1. Decide what you want to use as an instrument. Try one of the suggested objects or find something else.

2. Have everyone play their instruments to hear the sounds they make. Use mops and brooms to make **sweeping** sounds.

3. Hold metal lids and use sticks like drumsticks.

4. Turn buckets and bowls upside down to make drums!

5. Have one person start to play his or her instrument. Each person joins in until everyone is playing together.

6. Move, leap, hop, and spin to the beat. There is no right or wrong way to play and move. **Switch** instruments after playing for a while. Have fun and keep moving!

Ribbon Dance

Dance and twirl to the beat!

WHAT YOU NEED

paper towel tube
construction paper
clear tape
paper streamers
masking tape
tape measure
scissors
music player
favorite music

MUSCLES USED

leg
arm
shoulder

TIME

10-30 minutes

Make Ribbon Wands

1. Put a paper towel tube on a piece of colored paper. The paper should be as wide as the tube. Tape the edge of the paper to the tube.

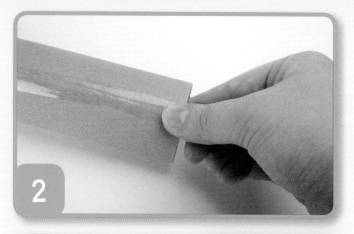

2. Wrap the paper around the tube. Tape the edge with clear tape.

3. Cut three paper streamers. Each streamer should be about 3 feet (1 to 1.2 m) long. Put masking tape on the end of each paper streamer.

4. Tape the ends of the streamers inside one end of the tube.

5. If you want, make a second **ribbon** rod. Then you can dance with one in each hand!

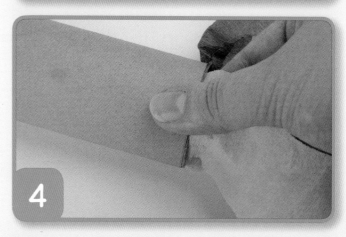

Ribbon Dance

1. Start the music. Move your arms and the streamers to the music.

2. Make big arm circles with both arms.

3. Hold both arms straight out. Move your arms up and down to make waves with the streamers. Make big waves and then make little waves.

4. Hold one **ribbon** rod with both hands. Twirl it over your head.

5. Make big figure eight movements. Try it over your head. Make them closer to the floor. Then go back up again.

6 Now add body movements. Bend forward and backward and side-to-side. Keep moving the **ribbon** rod with your arms.

7 Try moving your feet while twirling the ribbon rod. Step, jump, and kick to the beat!

8 Dance a ribbon dance by yourself or with friends! Dance to your favorite song. Keep your feet moving. Twirl the ribbons with your arms. Make sure your moves go with the music. Change the moves when the music changes. Now, practice, practice, practice!

Music March

March to the beat of your own drum!

WHAT YOU NEED

2 thick paper plates
markers
uncooked pasta
stapler
glue
scissors
ribbons
empty toilet paper tube
masking tape

MUSCLES USED

leg
arm

TIME

10-30 minutes

Paper Plate Tambourine

1 Put some uncooked pasta in one of the plates. Put the other plate upside-down on the first plate.

2 **Staple** the edges of the plates together.

3 Use markers to decorate the bottoms of the paper plates.

4 Glue pieces of **ribbon** around the edge. Shake your tambourine!

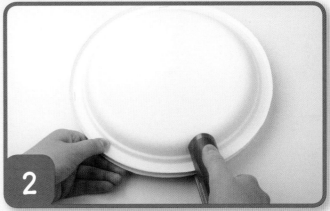

27

Toilet Paper Roll Shaker

1 Press the toilet paper tube flat. Cover one end with masking tape.

2 Put some uncooked pasta in the tube. Tape the tube closed.

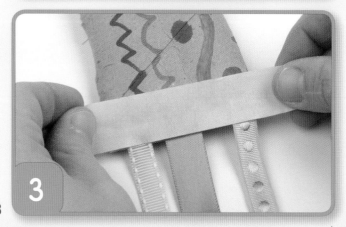

3 Decorate both sides with markers. Tape pieces of **ribbon** to each end.

4 Give your shaker a shake!

March!

1. Practice your instrument. How loud or soft can you shake it?

2. Choose someone to be the bandleader. Everyone lines up behind the leader.

3. The leader starts marching and shaking his or her instrument. Everyone follows the leader. Copy the way the leader moves and shakes the instrument.

4. Take turns being the bandleader.

5. Try different ways of marching and shaking. Lift your knees high, skip, jump.

Just Keep Moving!

Try these during TV and homework breaks, after meals, or anytime.

Limbo
Use a broom as a bar. Bend backwards and go under the bar. Each time drop the bar a little lower.

Rock Out
Put on your favorite pop or rock music. Keep dancing through the whole song. Have fun shaking and moving all parts of your body!

Dance Contest
Have everyone pick a different kind of music. Adults can teach kids the waltz, twist, or jitterbug. Kids can teach adults hip hop or line dancing.

Air Guitar
Pretend you are playing a guitar in a rock band. Jump, scream, swing your arms, and dance on a pretend stage.

Being active is for everyone!
- Ask your family to join in activities at home.
- Have relay races with your classmates at recess.
- Have an adult take you to a safe park to play tag with friends.

Super Simple Moves
Pledge

I promise to be active and move my body for one hour a day, five days a week.
I know that eating right and getting enough sleep are also important.
I want to be healthy and have a strong body.

I will:

☑ keep track of my activities on a Move It Chart or something like it

☑ ask my friends to stay active with me and set up play times outside three days a week

☑ ask my family to plan a physical activity one day a week

☑ limit my time watching TV and using the computer, except for homework

☑ get up and move my body during TV commercials and homework breaks

To print a pledge certificate, go to www.abdopublishing.com.
For more information about being active, please visit www.letsmove.gov.

31

Glossary

chore – a regular job or task, such as cleaning your room.

column – one of the vertical rows in a table or chart.

commercial – an ad that is on television or radio.

energy – the ability to move, work, or play hard without getting tired.

freeze – to become completely motionless.

muscle – the tissue connected to the bones that allows body parts to move.

punch – to hit with a closed fist.

ribbon – a long, narrow strip of material.

serving – a single portion of food.

staple – to fasten something together with a thin wire. The tool used to do this is called a *stapler*.

stomp – to step on something hard and suddenly.

sweep – to use a broom to clean or move something around.

switch – to change from one thing to another.

symbol – an object or picture that stands for or represents something.

verse – a part of a song or poem.